My Mind Is In A Fog What Do I Do?

Joshua Rhoades

Published by Joshua Paul Rhoades, 2024.

MY MIND IS IN A FOG WHAT DO I DO?

First edition. September 24, 2024.

Copyright © 2024 Joshua Rhoades.

ISBN: 979-8227018700

Written by Joshua Rhoades.

Also by Joshua Rhoades

Courage Under Fire: David's Stand On The Battlefield
Jonah's Journey: Voices Of Redemption And Lessons In Obedience
The Furnace Of Faith: 12 Principles From The Heat Of Faith
Whispers of Hope: Inspiring Stories of Men's Prayers In Scripture
Frontier Legends: The Oregon Dream
Elijah: A Beacon Of Boldness
HOOK, LINE & SAVIOUR - Faith Reflections from Fishing
Driven By Faith: Motor Racing Inspired Christian Life
30 Day Devotional - Bold and Strong- Coffee Devotions for a
Courageous Christian Walk
Authentic Christianity: The Heart of Old Time Religion
Consider The Ant - God's Tiny Preachers
Flee Fornication: The Plea For Purity
Renewed Hope- How to Find Encouragement in God
Sounding The Call - The Voice of Conviction
The Altar - Where Heaven Meets Earth
The Bible's Battlefields- Timeless Lessons from Ancient Wars
The Sacred Art of Silence - How Silence Speaks in Scripture
Under Fire- The Sanctity of the Traditional Biblical Home
Who Is on the Lord's Side? A Call to Righteousness
What Is Truth? - From Skepticism to Submission
First and Goal- Faith and Football Fundamentals
From Dugout to Devotion- Spiritual Lessons from Baseball
Par for the Course- Faith and Fairways
The Believer's Pace- Tools for Running Life's Marathon

The Immutable Fortress- Security in God's Unchanging Nature
Biblical Bravery
Deer Stands and Devotions: A Hunter's Walk with God
Jesus Knows- Our Hearts, Our Responsibility
Restoration - Setting The Bone
Spiritual 911- God's Word for Life's Emergency's
The Freedom of Forgiveness
The Jezebel Effect - Ancient Manipulations Modern Lessons
The Shout That Stopped The Saviour
The Time Machine Chronicles: Old Testament Characters
Anchored In Truth Exploring The Depths of Psalm 119
Biblical Counsel on Anger
Proverbs' Portraits The Men God Mentions
Stumbling in the Dark - The Dangers of Alcohol
Guarding the Wicket Protecting Your Faith and Game
The Champion's Faith - Wrestling and Achieving Spiritual Victory
Scriptural Commands for Modern Times Living God's Word Today
Volume 1
Scriptural Commands for Modern Times Living God's Word Today
Volume 2
Scriptural Commands for Modern Times Living God's Word
TodayVolume3
The Greatest Gift
A Christmas Journey of Faith
Daughter Of The King: Embracing Your Identity In Christ
Determination and Dedication Building Strong Faith As A Young Man
Walking Through Walls God's Power to Part the Storms of Life
David's Song Of Deliverance Praising God Through Every Storm
From Weakness to Warrior: Gideon's Transformation
Why Did Jesus Weep?
My Mind Is In A Fog What Do I Do?

Dedication

Dear Reader,

If you've picked up this book, I want you to know that you are seen, valued, and loved. You may be feeling overwhelmed right now, burdened by confusion, weighed down by a fog that has settled in your mind. Maybe life has thrown challenges your way that you didn't expect, or perhaps you're struggling to find clarity in the midst of uncertainty. Wherever you find yourself, you're not alone. I wrote this book with you in mind, and my prayer is that it will bring you the peace and encouragement your heart is yearning for.

I know what it's like to feel stuck in that fog—when every step forward feels heavy and every decision feels impossible. It can feel like you're walking through a thick haze, unable to see clearly or find your way out. I've been there, and I understand the frustration, the weariness, and the ache of not knowing what to do next. But even in those moments of uncertainty, there is hope. God is with you in the fog, even when it feels like you can't see Him or feel His presence.

This journey through the fog is not one you need to walk alone. God has promised never to leave or forsake you. Even in the darkest, most confusing times, He is guiding you, lighting your path one step at a time. The fog may feel overwhelming, but God is greater than anything you face. He holds you, your future, and your every worry in His hands. He knows exactly where you are, and He knows exactly how to lead you through.

If there's one thing I want you to take away from this book, it's this: you are not alone, and you do not have to have all the answers. It's okay to feel uncertain, it's okay to feel confused, and it's okay to feel weary. God's grace is sufficient for you, even in the fog. He invites you to rest in Him, to lean into His promises, and to trust that He is working things out for your good, even when you can't see it.

This book is an invitation to release your fears, worries, and burdens to the One who is never overwhelmed by them. It's an invitation to find peace in the middle of the storm, clarity in the midst of confusion, and hope when the path ahead feels uncertain. As you journey through these pages, I pray you will experience the powerful presence of God in a new and deeper way. May you feel His arms of love wrapped around you, comforting you and reminding you that you are His.

Dear reader, you are more resilient than you realize. The fog will not last forever. There will come a day when the clouds will part, and the path will become clear once again. Until that day, hold fast to the truth that God is guiding you, even when you can't see the way. You are precious to Him, and He will never let you go.

May this book bring you the encouragement and hope your heart needs. And may you walk through the fog with faith, trusting that God is leading you into a future filled with His peace, purpose, and love.

With all my heart,
Joshua Rhoades

Introduction

LIFE CAN OFTEN FEEL overwhelming, leaving us stuck in a mental fog where confusion, stress, and uncertainty cloud our thoughts. We might feel lost, unsure of how to move forward, or weighed down by the challenges in front of us. When our minds are in this fog, it can be hard to see clearly, make decisions, or even feel connected to God. But the good news is that we don't have to navigate this fog alone. God's Word offers us the clarity and guidance we need when everything feels overwhelming.

In "My Mind Is In A Fog, What Do I Do?", we explore how Scripture provides a roadmap to help us clear the mental fog and find peace in the midst of confusion. The Bible is filled with wisdom that speaks directly to the struggles we face when our minds feel clouded. Through passages of encouragement, and timeless principles, we'll uncover how God invites us to trust Him, renew our minds, and walk by faith, even when the path ahead isn't clear.

In Romans 12:2, we are called to "be transformed by the renewing of our mind," a reminder that God's Word has the power to clear away confusion and align our thoughts with His will. This book will show you how to renew your mind through Scripture, bringing clarity where there was once chaos. Whether it's through prayer, meditation on God's promises, or simply trusting Him with the unknown, we'll learn how to let go of the distractions and fears that weigh us down.

Additionally, 2 Corinthians 5:7 tells us to "walk by faith, not by sight," encouraging us to trust God even when we can't see the full picture. When our minds are foggy, it's easy to feel stuck, but faith empowers us to take the next step, trusting that God is guiding us. This book will explore how walking in faith helps us move forward when clarity seems out of reach, providing practical steps for trusting God in every circumstance.

This journey isn't about achieving perfect mental clarity overnight, but about learning how to walk with God through the fog. Psalm 46:10 reminds us to "Be still, and know that I am God." In moments of confusion, we can find peace in stillness, trusting that God is in control. As we quiet our minds and focus on His presence, we begin to see the fog lift, and we discover the clarity and peace that only He can provide.

Throughout this book, you will find scriptural support, practical advice, and personal reflections to help you navigate life's foggy moments with faith, hope, and trust in God. Whether you're feeling overwhelmed by life's demands, uncertain about the future, or simply in need of direction, "My Mind Is In A Fog, What Do I Do?" is a reminder that God is with you, guiding you through the fog, and leading you toward the clarity, peace, and purpose He has for your life.

Chapter 1 - Meditation

When your mind is in a fog, it feels like everything is blurry and unclear. You might be trying to focus, but it seems like your thoughts are scattered all over the place, making it hard to concentrate on anything important. It can feel overwhelming, like you're carrying a heavy weight, and no matter how hard you try, you can't seem to shake off the confusion. This is when turning to Psalm 1:2 can offer some much-needed help. The verse says, "But his delight is in the law of the LORD; and in his law doth he meditate day and night." This reminds us of the power of meditation on God's Word. Meditation is not just sitting quietly and doing nothing, but rather it's the act of focusing your mind on something meaningful—in this case, the teachings of God. When your thoughts are all over the place, instead of trying to solve everything at once, you can take a step back and focus on what really matters. Psalm 1:2 encourages us to meditate on God's law, meaning His teachings and promises. By doing so, we can shift our attention away from the overwhelming problems and thoughts that are clouding our minds and instead center our thoughts on the wisdom and guidance that God provides. When we delight in God's Word and meditate on it "day and night," as the verse says, we give our minds something steady and true to focus on. This process helps clear away the fog because it brings clarity, peace, and direction to our lives. The more we focus on God's promises, the more our minds begin to calm down, and the confusion starts to fade. Instead of being consumed by worries or stress, meditation on Scripture allows us to see things more clearly, helping us understand what is most important. It's like wiping away the fog from a window—suddenly, you can see things that were hidden or blurred before. Meditation on God's Word is like that for our minds. The more we meditate on His teachings, the clearer our thoughts become, and we are able to make better decisions, understand our emotions, and even feel a sense of peace that we didn't have before. Many times, the fog in our minds is caused by stress, anxiety, or the overwhelming feeling that we have too much on our plates. But when we meditate on Scripture, particularly verses like Psalm 1:2, we are reminded that we don't have to carry those burdens alone. God's Word provides comfort and wisdom that can guide us through even the most confusing and stressful times. It's easy to get lost in our own thoughts, especially when life feels chaotic, but Psalm 1:2 reminds us to focus on something bigger and more stable than our ever-changing emotions or circumstances. Meditation also takes practice. It's not something that will completely change your mindset overnight, but over time, the habit of regularly meditating on Scripture can lead to lasting changes in how you think and feel. When we make it a daily practice, as Psalm 1:2 suggests—meditating "day and night"—it starts to reshape the way we approach our problems. Instead of feeling overwhelmed by the fog, we can find peace in knowing that God's Word is constant and true, and it can guide us through any situation. In practical terms, meditation might look like spending a few minutes each morning reading a verse and thinking about how it applies to your life. It might mean pausing during a stressful day to remind yourself of God's promises. It could also mean ending your day by reflecting on how God has been present in your life, even in the small things. The more you make meditation a habit, the more it will help clear your mind. It's like training your brain to focus on what's important instead of getting lost in the noise of everything else. Psalm 1:2 doesn't just tell us to meditate for the sake of it—it shows us that delighting in God's Word is part of the process. This means finding joy in reading Scripture, learning from it, and applying it to our lives. When we find delight in something, it becomes easier to focus on it. So, the more we enjoy learning from God's Word, the more naturally meditation will come to us, and the clearer our minds will become over time. If you're feeling like your mind is in a fog, one of the best things you can do is turn to Scripture. Start with Psalm 1:2 and make a commitment to meditate on God's Word regularly. You'll find that as you do, the mental fog will start to lift, and you'll gain a clearer sense of purpose, direction, and peace in your life. You don't have to have all the answers right away, but meditation will help you focus on what really matters and allow God's Word to guide you through the confusion. It's a powerful tool that can transform not just your thoughts but your entire outlook on life. As you continue to meditate on God's Word, you'll find that the fog in your mind starts to clear, and you'll begin to see things with a new perspective, one that is grounded in truth and guided by God's wisdom.

Chapter 2 - Mindfulness

When your mind is in a fog, it can feel like everything is uncertain, and you don't know what to focus on or how to move forward. You might be worrying about things that haven't even happened yet, or you could be stressing about what tomorrow will bring. It's easy to get caught up in anxious thoughts about the future, which can make your mind feel even more clouded and confused. But in Matthew 6:34, Jesus tells us, "Take therefore no thought for the morrow: for the morrow shall take thought for the things of itself. Sufficient unto the day is the evil thereof." This verse is so powerful because it reminds us not to worry about what tomorrow might bring. Instead, we are called to focus on today and trust that God has the future in His hands. Worrying about the future can often be the main reason our minds feel foggy. We are so focused on what might happen, what could go wrong, or how things will turn out that we lose sight of what's right in front of us. Matthew 6:34 teaches us that we should not be consumed with tomorrow's troubles because each day has enough challenges of its own. This verse encourages us to live in the present and trust that God will take care of tomorrow, freeing our minds from unnecessary stress and worry. When we spend all our time thinking about the future, we lose the ability to focus on the present moment. Our minds become clouded with "what ifs" and worst-case scenarios, which can make it hard to think clearly or make good decisions. This is what it means to have a mind in a fog—when your thoughts are scattered, and you can't seem to find clarity. But when we apply the wisdom of Matthew 6:34, we are reminded that worrying about tomorrow won't help us today. In fact, it only makes things harder by adding to the mental fog. Jesus is telling us to stop wasting time and energy on things we cannot control. Instead, we should focus on the present moment and trust that God will handle the rest. The idea of mindfulness comes into play here. Mindfulness means being fully present and aware of what is happening right now, instead of letting your mind race ahead to the future. When Jesus says, "Take no thought for the morrow," He's encouraging us to practice mindfulness by focusing on today and trusting Him with what comes next. When you let go of future worries and focus on the present, it helps clear the mental fog because your mind isn't scattered between what's happening now and what might happen later. Living in the present doesn't mean ignoring your responsibilities or pretending that the future doesn't matter. It means trusting that God is in control and that you don't need to carry the weight of tomorrow's worries today. This shift in thinking can bring a lot of relief to a foggy mind. Imagine carrying a heavy backpack full of rocks—each rock represents a worry about the future. The more you think about the future, the more rocks you add to your backpack. Eventually, it becomes so heavy that you can't even walk straight, and your mind feels weighed down with stress. But Matthew 6:34 is like a reminder to take that backpack off and leave it at the feet of Jesus. You don't have to carry those burdens anymore because God is already handling them for you. This doesn't mean that life will always be easy or that we won't face challenges. Jesus acknowledges in this verse that "sufficient unto the day is the evil thereof," meaning that each day has its own struggles and difficulties. However, worrying about tomorrow only adds to today's burdens, making it even harder to deal with what's right in front of you. By focusing on the present, you are better able to handle today's challenges without the added weight of future worries clouding your mind. Another important point to take from this verse is the idea of trust. Letting go of future worries requires us to trust that God is in control and that He will provide for our needs. When we don't trust God, we feel like we have to figure everything out on our own, which can lead to even more stress and anxiety. But when we trust that God has our future in His hands, it becomes easier to focus on today and let go of the things we can't control. This trust in God is essential for clearing the mental fog because it shifts our focus away from the uncertainties of the future and back to the certainty of God's care and provision. The mental fog often comes from fear—fear of the unknown, fear of failure, fear of what tomorrow will bring. But Matthew 6:34 is a reminder that we don't need to live in fear. God is already in our tomorrow, and He knows what we need. Instead of being consumed by fear and worry, we can rest in the knowledge that God is taking care of us, both today and tomorrow. This trust in God's provision is the key to finding peace in the present moment. When we trust that God will take care of tomorrow, we are free to focus on what really matters today. This doesn't mean that we won't face challenges or that everything will always go according to plan. But it does mean that we don't have to carry the weight of future worries on our own. God is with us, and He will provide what we need, one day at a time. Another thing to consider is how living in the present can actually help us make better decisions for the future. When our minds are in a fog, we often make decisions based on fear or worry about what might happen. But when we focus on the present and trust God with the future, we are able to make clearer, more thoughtful decisions. We can approach life with a sense of peace and confidence, knowing that God is guiding us. This mindset shift can have a profound impact on our mental clarity. Instead of feeling overwhelmed by the unknown, we can find peace in the present moment, trusting that God will take care of the rest. It's important to remember that living in the present is a daily practice. It's not something that happens automatically, especially if you're used to worrying about the future. It takes intentional effort to focus on today and trust God with tomorrow. But the more you practice this, the more natural it will become. Over time, you'll find that the mental fog starts to lift, and you'll be able to approach life with a clearer mind and a greater sense of peace. One practical way to apply this principle is to start each day by focusing on what you can do today, rather than worrying about what might happen tomorrow. You can pray and ask God for guidance for today's challenges, trusting that He will provide what you need when tomorrow comes. By making this a habit, you'll begin to see a difference in how you approach life. Instead of being overwhelmed by the future, you'll be able to focus on the present and trust that God is handling the rest. In conclusion, when your mind is in a fog, one of the best things you can do is apply the wisdom of Matthew 6:34. By focusing on today and trusting God with tomorrow, you can clear the mental fog and find peace in the present moment. This doesn't mean that life will always be easy or that we won't face challenges. But it does mean that we don't have to carry the weight of tomorrow's worries today. God is in control, and He will provide for our needs, one day at a time. When we live in the present and trust God with the future, we are able to approach life with a clearer mind and a greater sense of peace. So, take a deep breath, let go of future worries, and trust that God is already in your tomorrow, working everything out for your good.

Chapter 3 - Mentorship

When your mind is in a fog, it can feel like you're lost in a maze with no clear way out. Thoughts may be swirling around in your head, and it becomes hard to make decisions or know what steps to take next. You might feel stuck, overwhelmed, and unsure of what to do. This mental fog can be frustrating and even scary at times, especially when important decisions need to be made or when life is pulling you in multiple directions. Proverbs 11:14 gives us wise advice for these moments when it says, "Where no counsel is, the people fall: but in the multitude of counsellors there is safety." This verse reminds us that we don't have to navigate life's challenges alone. Seeking wise counsel, or mentorship, can be the key to clearing the fog in our minds and finding the clarity we need. When we feel confused or lost, it's often because we're trying to figure everything out on our own. The weight of making decisions, solving problems, or planning for the future can feel overwhelming, and this is when our minds start to get cloudy. We may second-guess ourselves, worry about making the wrong choice, or get stuck in a cycle of indecision. This is exactly when seeking guidance from others can make a huge difference. Proverbs 11:14 shows us that there is wisdom in seeking counsel from those who have experience and knowledge. Just like a coach helps an athlete improve their performance, or a teacher guides a student through difficult lessons, mentors or wise counselors can offer valuable perspectives that help us see things more clearly. When we are in the middle of mental fog, our own perspective can be limited. We might be too close to the problem to see all the options, or we may be blinded by our own worries and fears. A mentor or counselor can offer an outside perspective, which often helps us realize things we couldn't see on our own. Their wisdom can cut through the confusion and bring much-needed clarity. Think about how much easier it is to solve a puzzle when someone else points out a piece you missed or shows you a different way to look at the problem. That's what mentorship is like. It brings fresh insights and can make a complicated situation seem more manageable. The verse from Proverbs also emphasizes that "in the multitude of counsellors there is safety." This means that it's not just about asking one person for advice but surrounding yourself with a variety of voices that offer wisdom. When we consult different people—whether it's a parent, teacher, pastor, or trusted friend—we gather a range of perspectives that can help us make more informed and confident decisions. The more wise counsel we seek, the more likely we are to find the answers we need. This also protects us from making rash or unwise decisions that could lead to regret. The safety mentioned in this verse comes from knowing that we are not making decisions in isolation but with the support and guidance of others who care about us and have our best interests in mind. When our minds are foggy, it's easy to feel alone, like no one understands what we're going through. But seeking counsel reminds us that we are not alone in our struggles. There are people who have gone through similar experiences, and their wisdom can help guide us through the fog. A mentor who has faced similar challenges can share how they overcame them, offering hope and encouragement. Their experience can shine a light on the path ahead, helping us avoid common mistakes and showing us the best way forward. Mentorship is also about learning from others' mistakes and successes. When we're stuck in mental fog, we might be afraid of making the wrong decision or taking the wrong step. But hearing about how others have navigated similar situations can give us the confidence to move forward. Their stories remind us that we're not the first to face challenges, and we won't be the last. There is comfort in knowing that others have made it through, and we can too. Another important part of mentorship is accountability. When our minds are foggy, it's easy to procrastinate or avoid making decisions because we're unsure of what to do. A mentor or wise counselor can provide gentle accountability, encouraging us to take action even when we feel stuck. They can help us break down overwhelming tasks into smaller, more manageable steps. This can be incredibly helpful when our minds are clouded by confusion or worry. Having someone to check in with can motivate us to keep moving forward, even when we don't feel like it. Proverbs 11:14 reminds us that without counsel, people fall. This speaks to the danger of trying to figure everything out on our own. When we're in a mental fog, our judgment can be clouded, and we may not always make the best decisions. This is when we're most at risk of falling—falling into bad decisions, falling into worry and stress, or falling away from the right path. But with wise counsel, there is safety. Mentors and counselors can help us avoid pitfalls and guide us toward better choices. They act like guardrails on a winding road, keeping us from veering off course when we can't see clearly. The safety that comes from seeking counsel isn't just about avoiding mistakes; it's also about finding peace of mind. When we're in a fog, our minds are often filled with worry and uncertainty. But when we talk to someone who has been through it before, or someone who has the wisdom we need, it brings a sense of calm. We realize that we don't have to have all the answers right now and that it's okay to lean on others for support. This brings peace and helps lift the mental fog. It's important to remember that not all advice is created equal. Proverbs 11:14 talks about wise counsel, which means we need to be careful about who we turn to for advice. The best mentors and counselors are those who share our values, have experience, and genuinely care about our well-being. Seeking advice from someone who lacks these qualities might only add to our confusion. But when we seek out those who are wise, experienced, and trustworthy, we are more likely to find the clarity we need. One way to find wise counsel is through prayer. Asking God to guide us to the right people can open doors to mentorship we may not have considered. Sometimes the person who offers the most helpful advice is someone we didn't expect—a teacher, a family friend, or even a coworker. God often places people in our lives at just the right time to offer the counsel we need. Another benefit of mentorship is that it helps us grow. When we seek counsel, we open ourselves up to learning from others, which helps us grow in wisdom and understanding. Each time we ask for advice or listen to someone's guidance, we learn something new that we can apply to our own life. Over time, these lessons add up, helping us navigate future challenges with more confidence and clarity. So, when your mind is in a fog, and you don't know what to do, remember the wisdom of Proverbs 11:14. Don't try to figure it all out on your own. Seek out wise counsel and surround yourself with people who can offer guidance, support, and accountability. Their wisdom can help clear the fog, making it easier to see the path ahead. Whether it's a mentor, a pastor, a family member, or a trusted friend, their advice can provide the clarity you need to make decisions with confidence. In the multitude of counsellors, there is safety, and that safety brings peace, clarity, and direction in times of mental fog.

Chapter 4 - Motivation from Scripture

When your mind is in a fog, it can feel like you're stuck in a thick cloud, unable to think clearly or make sense of what's going on around you. It's as if everything that should be simple becomes complicated, and every decision seems harder than it needs to be. This feeling of mental fog can come from stress, worry, exhaustion, or feeling overwhelmed by life's challenges. It's easy to feel like you're powerless to break through it. But in times like these, it's important to remember the powerful truth found in Philippians 4:13, which says, "I can do all things through Christ which strengtheneth me." This verse is a source of incredible motivation and strength because it reminds us that we are not relying on our own abilities or strength to get through tough times. Instead, we can lean on Christ, who gives us the strength we need to overcome any challenge, even when our minds feel foggy and unclear. Sometimes, when we're in the middle of a mental fog, it can seem impossible to move forward. We might feel stuck, like there's no way out of the confusion. But Philippians 4:13 reminds us that no matter how difficult things seem, Christ is our source of strength. It's not about how strong or smart we are; it's about trusting in the strength that Christ gives us. When we rely on His strength, we can do things we never thought were possible. We can find clarity in the midst of confusion, hope in the midst of despair, and peace in the midst of chaos. This verse is a reminder that we don't have to fight our battles alone. We don't have to figure everything out by ourselves. Christ is with us, giving us the strength and wisdom we need to break through the mental fog and see things clearly again. One of the reasons our minds often feel foggy is because we're trying to carry too much on our own. We try to handle every problem, worry, and fear by ourselves, and it becomes too much to bear. This is when mental clarity starts to slip away, and everything feels overwhelming. But Philippians 4:13 tells us that we don't have to carry these burdens on our own. Christ is there to strengthen us, to help us carry the load, and to give us the ability to keep going even when it feels impossible. When we remember that Christ is the source of our strength, it changes the way we approach challenges. Instead of feeling defeated or overwhelmed, we can face each day with confidence, knowing that we are not alone. Christ is with us, and He is giving us the strength to overcome whatever comes our way. This truth can clear the fog in our minds because it shifts our focus away from our own limitations and onto the limitless power of Christ. Another reason why Philippians 4:13 is so powerful is that it reminds us that we can do "all things" through Christ. This means that no challenge is too big for Him to handle, and there's no situation that's too complicated for Him to guide us through. Whether it's a difficult decision, a stressful situation, or a personal struggle, Christ is more than capable of helping us through it. He gives us the strength to tackle the hard things, and He gives us the wisdom to see things clearly, even when our minds feel clouded. When we're in the middle of a mental fog, it's easy to forget this. It's easy to feel like we're stuck and there's no way out. But Philippians 4:13 reminds us that with Christ, we are never truly stuck. He is always with us, giving us the strength we need to take the next step, even when we don't know what that step looks like. Mental fog can make us feel powerless, but this verse reminds us that we are not powerless. Through Christ, we have the power to overcome anything that comes our way. Sometimes, we feel like we can't move forward because we don't have all the answers. We want to wait until the fog clears completely before we make a decision or take action. But Philippians 4:13 encourages us to trust in Christ's strength even when we don't have all the answers. We don't have to wait for everything to be perfect or clear before we move forward. Christ gives us the strength to keep going, even when things are still uncertain. He gives us the courage to take the next step, trusting that He will guide us through the fog and lead us to clarity. This is why Philippians 4:13 is such a powerful motivator. It reminds us that Christ's strength is always available to us, no matter what we're facing. We don't have to wait until we feel strong or capable on our own. We can rely on Christ's strength right now, in the middle of the fog, and trust that He will help us find our way. When we focus on this truth, it helps to clear the mental fog because it gives us a sense of purpose and direction. We stop feeling stuck and start feeling empowered, knowing that we can do all things through Christ who strengthens us. It's also important to remember that Philippians 4:13 doesn't just apply to the big challenges in life. It applies to everything, including the small, everyday struggles that can add up and contribute to mental fog. Whether it's dealing with stress at work, managing responsibilities at home, or simply trying to stay focused during a busy day, Christ is there to give us the strength we need. We can turn to Him for help in every situation, trusting that He will give us the clarity and peace we need to keep moving forward. When we meditate on this verse and let it sink into our hearts, it can have a profound impact on the way we think and feel. Instead of feeling overwhelmed by life's challenges, we start to see them as opportunities to rely on Christ's strength. Instead of feeling powerless, we start to feel empowered, knowing that we can do all things through Christ. This shift in perspective can help to clear the mental fog and bring a sense of peace and confidence that we may have been missing. It's also helpful to remember that Philippians 4:13 is not just about physical strength. It's about emotional and mental strength as well. When our minds are in a fog, it's often because we're carrying a lot of emotional weight—worry, fear, stress, or anxiety. But Christ's strength is available to help us with these things too. He can give us the emotional and mental strength we need to face our challenges with peace and clarity. When we feel like we're at the end of our rope, when we feel like we can't handle one more thing, we can turn to Christ and ask for His strength. And He will give it to us. Philippians 4:13 is a promise that we can hold onto in times of mental fog. It's a reminder that no matter how difficult things get, we are not alone. Christ is with us, giving us the strength we need to overcome every challenge. Whether it's a small obstacle or a big life decision, we can trust that Christ will give us the wisdom, clarity, and strength we need to move forward. So, when your mind is in a fog and you don't know what to do, remember Philippians 4:13. Remind yourself that you can do all things through Christ who strengthens you. Turn to Him for help, and trust that He will give you the strength and clarity you need to break through the fog and find your way forward. You don't have to rely on your own strength, because Christ's strength is more than enough. He will guide you, strengthen you, and give you the peace and clarity you need to overcome any challenge. Trust in Him, and you will find that the fog begins to lift, and you will be able to see the path ahead with fresh eyes and a renewed sense of hope.

Chapter 5 - Mental Decluttering

When your mind is in a fog, everything can feel messy, overwhelming, and out of control. You might have a hundred thoughts racing through your head, making it hard to focus on any one thing. You might feel like you're trying to juggle too many tasks at once, and none of them seem to be getting done. It's easy to get caught up in the chaos of life, and when your thoughts are cluttered, it can make everything seem more difficult than it really is. This is when mental fog sets in, clouding your ability to think clearly and make good decisions. But the Bible gives us a simple and powerful principle to help clear this mental clutter and bring order to our minds. In 1 Corinthians 14:40, it says, "Let all things be done decently and in order." This verse speaks directly to the need for organization and structure in our lives, both in the physical sense and in our thoughts. When we bring order to the chaos around us, it becomes much easier to think clearly and manage the tasks in front of us. One of the reasons we often experience mental fog is that our minds are overloaded with too many things at once. We have responsibilities at home, school, work, and in our relationships, and sometimes it feels like everything is happening all at once. This can create a cluttered mind, where it's hard to know where to start or what to focus on first. But 1 Corinthians 14:40 reminds us that God values order, and this is something we can apply to our own lives. By bringing order to the chaos, we can start to clear away the mental fog that is keeping us from being productive and at peace. The first step to clearing mental clutter is to take a look at what's going on in your life. Are there too many things pulling at your attention? Are you trying to do too much at once?

Sometimes, the fog in our minds is a result of trying to multitask, which can actually make us less efficient and more overwhelmed. Instead of doing everything at once, we can follow the advice in 1 Corinthians 14:40 and bring order to our tasks by focusing on one thing at a time. Prioritizing our responsibilities can help bring clarity to our thoughts. Start by writing down everything that's on your mind, everything that's stressing you out or causing you to feel overwhelmed. Once you have it all in front of you, it's easier to organize it into smaller, more manageable tasks. This simple act of getting your thoughts out of your head and onto paper can immediately help clear away some of the fog. When everything is swirling around in your mind, it's hard to know where to start, but when it's written down, you can begin to see a clear path forward. After you've written everything down, you can begin to prioritize. What are the most important things that need to be done today? What can wait until later? By focusing on the most urgent or important tasks first, you can start to tackle the mental clutter in a way that feels more manageable. Trying to do everything at once often leads to burnout and confusion, but when you organize your tasks and take them one at a time, it becomes much easier to think clearly and stay focused. This is the principle of doing things "decently and in order," as 1 Corinthians 14:40 instructs. It's about taking a chaotic situation and bringing structure to it, which in turn helps to bring peace to your mind. Another important aspect of mental decluttering is learning to let go of things that are not necessary. Sometimes, the mental fog we experience is because we are holding on to too many worries or responsibilities that we don't really need to carry. It's like trying to carry a backpack that is overloaded with stuff you don't need—it slows you down and makes it harder to move forward. But when you follow the advice of 1 Corinthians 14:40 and bring order to your thoughts, you can start to let go of the things that are weighing you down. Ask yourself, "Do I really need to be worrying about this right now?" or "Is this something I can delegate or let go of?" By getting rid of unnecessary worries or tasks, you free up mental space to focus on what really matters. This process of decluttering your mind helps to lift the fog and make things clearer. It's also important to remember that bringing order to your life doesn't just apply to tasks and responsibilities. It also applies to your thoughts and emotions. Sometimes, mental fog is caused by emotional clutter—worries, fears, or negative thoughts that are swirling around in your head. These thoughts can take up a lot of mental energy and make it hard to focus on anything else. But just like we can bring order to our tasks, we can also bring order to our thoughts. When negative or unhelpful thoughts start to take over, we can remind ourselves of the truth of God's Word and refocus our minds on what is good, true, and helpful. Philippians 4:8 tells us to think on things that are true, honest, just, pure, lovely, and of good report. By focusing on these things, we can declutter our minds from the negative thoughts that are contributing to our mental fog. Another way to bring order to your thoughts is through prayer and meditation on Scripture. When life feels chaotic and your mind is clouded with too many things, taking time to pray and reflect on God's Word can help bring peace and clarity. Prayer is a way of handing over your worries and stresses to God, trusting that He is in control and will guide you through whatever challenges you are facing. Meditation on Scripture, like the verse from 1 Corinthians 14:40, helps to remind us of the importance of order and peace in our lives. When we meditate on God's Word, it helps to refocus our minds on what truly matters, clearing away the clutter of unnecessary worries and fears. Decluttering your mind isn't something that happens overnight, but it's a process that can bring lasting peace and clarity. It starts with recognizing that your mind is overloaded and taking steps to bring order to the chaos. Whether it's organizing your tasks, letting go of unnecessary worries, or refocusing your thoughts on what is true and helpful, each step you take to declutter your mind helps to clear away the fog. 1 Corinthians 14:40 is a powerful reminder that God values order, and when we bring order to our lives, it brings peace to our minds. When everything around us feels chaotic, and our minds are clouded with too many thoughts, it can be hard to feel at peace. But when we follow the principle of doing things "decently and in order," we create space for peace and clarity to enter our lives. Organizing your thoughts and responsibilities isn't just about being more productive—it's about finding peace in the midst of life's chaos. It's about creating a sense of order that allows you to focus on what truly matters and let go of the things that are causing unnecessary stress. When your mind is in a fog, it can feel like you're spinning your wheels, trying to move forward but not getting anywhere. But when you take the time to declutter your mind and bring order to your life, the fog starts to lift, and you can see the path ahead more clearly. You don't have to live in a constant state of mental fog. By applying the wisdom of 1 Corinthians 14:40, you can take control of the chaos in your life and find the peace and clarity that comes from living in order. It's not always easy, but with practice, you can develop habits that help you stay organized and focused, even when life feels overwhelming. Whether it's creating a to-do list, setting aside time for prayer and reflection, or simply letting go of unnecessary worries, each step you take toward decluttering your mind helps to clear the mental fog and bring order to your life. So, when your mind is in a fog and everything feels overwhelming, remember the words of 1 Corinthians 14:40: "Let all things be done decently and in order." Take a deep breath, and start organizing your thoughts and tasks, one step at a time. As you bring order to your life, the mental fog will begin to lift, and you'll be able to think more clearly and approach life's challenges with a renewed sense of peace and purpose. You don't have to be stuck in the fog. With God's help and the wisdom of His Word, you can declutter your mind and find the clarity you need to move forward with confidence and peace.

Chapter 6 - Morning Routine

When your mind is in a fog, it can be hard to start your day on the right foot. Everything feels jumbled, and your thoughts are scattered, making it difficult to focus or figure out what needs to be done. Mental fog often makes even simple tasks seem overwhelming, and it can leave you feeling stuck and unsure of how to move forward. This is why having a solid morning routine, grounded in time with God, can be a powerful way to clear the fog and set the tone for the rest of the day. Psalm 5:3 says, "My voice shalt thou hear in the morning, O LORD; in the morning will I direct my prayer unto thee, and will look up." This verse reminds us of the importance of starting each day with prayer and looking up to God for guidance. When you begin your morning by focusing on God, it can bring clarity and peace to your mind, helping to lift the fog that might be clouding your thoughts. One of the reasons our minds often feel foggy is because we're overwhelmed by all the things we need to do. We wake up thinking about everything that's on our plate—school, work, family responsibilities, and personal worries. This flood of thoughts can make it hard to get started, and before you know it, you're stuck in a cycle of stress and confusion. But when you take the time to pray and seek God first thing in the morning, you're able to hand over those worries to Him. You're reminded that you don't have to carry the weight of the day on your own. By starting your day with prayer, as Psalm 5:3 encourages, you're inviting God into every part of your day and asking Him to help you navigate through it with clarity and purpose. Establishing a morning routine that includes prayer and reflection can help you break through the mental fog because it gives you a sense of direction. Instead of waking up and immediately feeling overwhelmed, you can approach the day with confidence, knowing that you've taken the time to seek God's guidance. This sense of direction is crucial when your mind is foggy because it provides a clear starting point. You're no longer wandering through the day, unsure of what to focus on or how to handle the challenges ahead. Instead, you've set the tone for the day by putting God first and trusting Him to lead you. Another reason why a morning routine is so effective at clearing mental fog is that it creates a sense of structure. Mental fog often thrives in chaos—when your thoughts are all over the place, and you don't have a plan, it's easy to feel lost and confused. But by establishing a routine that begins with time spent in prayer and reading Scripture, you create a sense of order in your day. This structure helps to clear the mental clutter because it allows you to focus on what's most important. You're no longer trying to juggle everything at once; instead, you're taking things one step at a time, with God at the center of it all. Psalm 5:3 emphasizes the idea of looking up to God in the morning, which is a powerful reminder to shift your focus away from the problems and stresses of the day and instead focus on God's presence and guidance. When your mind is in a fog, it's easy to get caught up in everything that's going wrong or everything that needs to be done. But by taking a moment each morning to look up to God, you're reminded that He is in control and that you don't have to figure everything out on your own. This shift in focus can bring a sense of peace and clarity that helps to break through the mental fog. Another benefit of starting your day with prayer is that it helps you prioritize. When your mind is foggy, it can be hard to know what to focus on first. You might feel pulled in a million different directions, unsure of where to start. But when you take the time to pray in the morning, you're able to ask God for wisdom and guidance on what's most important. This helps you prioritize your tasks and responsibilities in a way that aligns with God's will. Instead of trying to do everything at once, you can focus on the things that matter most, which helps to reduce the feeling of being overwhelmed. Prayer also has a calming effect on the mind. When you're in a mental fog, it's easy to feel anxious or stressed about the day ahead. But prayer is a way to release that anxiety and find peace in God's presence. Psalm 5:3 reminds us that when we direct our prayers to God in the morning, we can look up with hope and trust that He is listening and will provide for us. This sense of peace and assurance can help clear away the mental fog, allowing you to approach the day with a calm and focused mind. One of the most powerful aspects of a morning routine grounded in prayer is that it helps you start the day with a positive mindset. Mental fog often brings with it negative thoughts—worry, doubt, fear, and frustration. These thoughts can cloud your judgment and make it hard to think clearly. But when you start your day by focusing on God's goodness and faithfulness, it shifts your mindset from negative to positive. You're reminded of His promises and His love for you, which brings a sense of hope and encouragement. This positive mindset helps to lift the fog and gives you the mental clarity you need to tackle the day's challenges. In addition to prayer, incorporating time for reflection or reading Scripture in your morning routine can also help clear mental fog. Reflecting on God's Word, even for just a few minutes, can provide valuable insights and encouragement that help you face the day with confidence. Scripture has a way of speaking directly to our hearts, offering comfort and wisdom that we might not have been able to see on our own. By taking the time to read and reflect on a verse or passage, you're giving your mind the space to process and gain clarity. This can be especially helpful when your thoughts feel scattered or unclear. Psalm 5:3 emphasizes the importance of seeking God in the morning, and this practice can have a profound impact on your mental and emotional well-being. When you make it a habit to start your day with prayer and reflection, it becomes easier to navigate through the fog of confusion or stress. You're no longer relying on your own strength or trying to figure everything out on your own. Instead, you're trusting God to guide you, and that trust brings peace, clarity, and direction. A morning routine that includes time with God also sets a spiritual tone for the rest of your day. It helps you stay connected to Him throughout the day, even when things get busy or stressful. When you start your day in prayer, it's easier to turn to God when challenges arise later on. You've already invited Him into your day, so when the mental fog starts to creep back in, you can quickly refocus and remember that God is with you. This ongoing connection to God helps to keep the fog at bay, allowing you to think more clearly and make better decisions throughout the day. Creating a morning routine that centers around prayer and time with God doesn't have to be complicated. It can be as simple as spending a few minutes in prayer as soon as you wake up or reading a short passage of Scripture before you start your day. The key is consistency—making it a daily habit that helps you start each day with a clear mind and a focused heart. Over time, this practice will become second nature, and you'll find that the mental fog you once struggled with becomes less and less of an issue. In conclusion, when your mind is in a fog, one of the best ways to find clarity is by establishing a morning routine that includes time spent with God. Psalm 5:3 encourages us to direct our prayers to God in the morning and look up to Him for guidance. When we start our day with prayer, we invite God into every part of our day, and this brings a sense of peace and clarity that helps to lift the mental fog. By creating a routine that focuses on prayer, reflection, and seeking God's guidance, we can bring order to the chaos in our minds and set the tone for a productive and peaceful day. Whether it's taking a few minutes to pray, reading a Bible verse, or simply reflecting on God's presence in your life, these small but powerful practices can have a big impact on your mental clarity and emotional well-being. You don't have to let mental fog control your day. By starting your morning with God, you can find the clarity, peace, and direction you need to move forward with confidence.

Chapter 7 - Mental Health Check

When your mind is in a fog, it can feel like you're carrying a heavy load that slows you down and clouds your ability to think clearly. Everything feels overwhelming, decisions seem harder, and it's as if your thoughts are spinning in circles without getting anywhere. This is a common experience when you're mentally or emotionally exhausted, stressed, or anxious, and it can affect every part of your life. But the good news is that Jesus offers an answer for those who feel burdened by life's challenges and mental struggles. In Matthew 11:28, Jesus says, "Come unto me, all ye that labour and are heavy laden, and I will give you rest." This verse offers a beautiful and powerful invitation to anyone who feels overwhelmed, mentally drained, or weighed down by life's pressures. When you're in the middle of mental fog, this invitation to come to Jesus and find rest is exactly what you need.

Mental fog often comes from trying to carry too much on your own. You might be dealing with stress at work, responsibilities at home, worries about the future, or personal struggles that weigh heavily on your mind. Over time, these burdens build up, and it becomes harder and harder to focus, think clearly, or feel at peace. It's like carrying a backpack that gets heavier with every new worry or responsibility, until it's so heavy that you can barely move. This is why checking in with your mental health is so important. You need to recognize when you're carrying too much, and you need to seek the rest and peace that Jesus offers. Matthew 11:28 reminds us that we don't have to carry these burdens alone—Jesus invites us to bring them to Him and find the rest we so desperately need.

One of the reasons mental fog can be so difficult to deal with is because we often try to push through it without taking the time to rest or recharge. We live in a world that values constant productivity, and there's often pressure to keep going, even when we're feeling mentally and emotionally exhausted. But this only makes the fog worse. When you don't take the time to rest, your mind becomes more and more cluttered, making it harder to focus, think clearly, or make good decisions. This is where the invitation from Jesus in Matthew 11:28 becomes so important. Jesus doesn't ask us to keep pushing through on our own strength. Instead, He invites us to come to Him, to lay down our burdens, and to find the rest that we need. This rest isn't just physical—it's a deep, spiritual rest that refreshes our minds and souls, bringing clarity and peace in the midst of life's chaos.

Checking in with your mental health is crucial because it helps you recognize when you need to take a step back and seek that rest. When you're in a mental fog, it's easy to ignore how much stress or anxiety you're carrying because you're focused on trying to get things done or keep up with your responsibilities. But ignoring your mental health only makes things worse in the long run. It's important to take a moment to pause, reflect, and ask yourself, "How am I really doing?" This kind of mental health check helps you recognize when you're carrying too much and need to come to Jesus for rest. It's a way of being honest with yourself and admitting that you need help, and that's okay. Jesus knows your struggles, and He wants to give you the rest and peace that your mind and heart need.

One of the most comforting things about Matthew 11:28 is that it shows us that we don't have to have everything figured out before we come to Jesus. He doesn't say, "Come to me when you've solved all your problems" or "Come to me when you're strong enough to carry your burdens." Instead, He invites us to come to Him exactly as we are—tired, burdened, and overwhelmed. When your mind is in a fog and you don't know what to do, Jesus is there, waiting for you to come to

Him so He can give you rest. This rest isn't just about taking a break from your responsibilities; it's about finding true peace and clarity in Him. It's about trusting that He can handle the burdens that are too heavy for you to carry on your own.

Rest is essential for mental clarity. When you're constantly going and never taking time to rest, your mind becomes overworked, and it's harder to think clearly. Rest allows your mind to recharge and process everything that's been weighing it down. But the rest that Jesus offers goes beyond just taking a nap or a day off. It's a deeper rest that comes from trusting Him with your worries, fears, and anxieties. When you bring your burdens to Jesus and trust Him to take care of them, it frees up mental space that was previously cluttered with stress. This kind of rest brings a sense of peace and calm that helps to clear the fog in your mind, making it easier to focus and make decisions.

Jesus understands what it's like to be weary and burdened. He knows the pressures and struggles of life, and He cares about your mental health. That's why He offers this invitation to come to Him for rest. It's not just an empty promise—it's a real, tangible offer of peace and clarity for anyone who feels weighed down by life. When you take the time to come to Jesus, to bring your mental and emotional struggles to Him, He responds with love and compassion. He doesn't turn you away or tell you to figure it out on your own. Instead, He meets you right where you are, offering you the rest and peace that only He can give.

Sometimes, mental fog comes from trying to control things that are out of your control. You might be worried about the future, stressed about things that haven't even happened yet, or trying to fix problems that are too big for you to handle on your own. But Jesus invites you to let go of those worries and trust Him. When you come to Him and lay down your burdens, you're acknowledging that you can't do it all on your own—and that's okay. Jesus is more than capable of carrying the burdens that are too heavy for you. When you release control and trust Him, it brings a sense of relief and clarity. The fog in your mind starts to lift because you're no longer trying to carry the weight of the world on your own shoulders.

In a world that often glorifies busyness and productivity, it's easy to feel guilty for needing rest. But rest is not a weakness—it's a necessity. Jesus Himself took time to rest and recharge, and He invites us to do the same. Mental health checks are an important part of taking care of yourself, and they allow you to recognize when you're running on empty and need to seek rest in Christ. When you take the time to check in with yourself and bring your burdens to Jesus, you're allowing Him to refresh your mind and soul, which in turn helps you think more clearly and approach life's challenges with a renewed sense of purpose.

It's important to remember that mental health is not just about avoiding burnout or exhaustion. It's about maintaining a sense of balance and peace in your life. When your mind is constantly filled with stress, worry, or anxiety, it's hard to function at your best. That's why coming to Jesus for rest is so important. He helps to restore that balance by giving you the peace and clarity you need to navigate life's ups and downs. Checking in with your mental health is a way of recognizing when you need to step back and allow Jesus to take the lead. It's about trusting that He knows what's best for you and that He will provide the rest and guidance you need.

The rest that Jesus offers in Matthew 11:28 is not just a temporary fix for when you're feeling overwhelmed—it's a lasting source of peace and strength. When you come to Him and bring your burdens, He doesn't just give you a momentary break from the chaos of life. He offers a deeper rest that transforms the way you approach your challenges. This rest brings a sense of calm and clarity that helps you see things more clearly and make decisions with confidence. It helps to lift the mental fog that has been clouding your mind, allowing you to move forward with a renewed sense of purpose and direction.

In conclusion, when your mind is in a fog, and you're feeling overwhelmed by life's challenges, the most important thing you can do is take a mental health check and come to Jesus for rest. Matthew 11:28 offers a beautiful invitation to anyone who is weary and burdened to find rest in Christ. This rest is not just physical—it's a deep, spiritual rest that brings peace and clarity to your mind and soul. By checking in with yourself and recognizing when you need to step back and seek rest in Jesus, you allow Him to carry your burdens and refresh your spirit. The mental fog begins to lift as you trust Him with your worries and anxieties, and you're able to approach life's challenges with a clearer mind and a sense of peace. So, when you feel weighed down and mentally exhausted, remember the words of Jesus: "Come unto me, all ye that labour and are heavy laden, and I will give you rest." Trust in His promise, and you will find the rest and clarity you need to move forward with confidence and peace.

Chapter 8 - Memory of God's Faithfulness

When your mind is in a fog, it feels like you're lost in a thick cloud, struggling to see clearly, and unsure of which way to go. It's a disorienting feeling, and it can leave you overwhelmed, anxious, and confused. Whether you're dealing with stress, grief, worry, or uncertainty, this mental fog makes it hard to focus, make decisions, or even feel like yourself. But when everything feels unclear, one of the most powerful things you can do is remember the faithfulness of God. In Lamentations 3:21-22, we find a powerful reminder of how God's mercies are always present, even in the darkest times. The verse says, "This I recall to my mind, therefore have I hope. It is of the LORD's mercies that we are not consumed, because his compassions fail not." These words were spoken during a time of immense suffering and despair, but they offer a beacon of hope that shines through the fog of confusion and uncertainty. When you feel lost in a mental fog, recalling God's faithfulness and mercy can bring clarity, peace, and a renewed sense of hope.

One of the reasons we often feel stuck in a mental fog is because we're focused on the problems and challenges in front of us. The weight of life's difficulties can feel overwhelming, and it becomes easy to forget that God has been with us through every storm and struggle we've faced before. But Lamentations 3:21 reminds us of the importance of remembering. "This I recall to my mind," the verse says, pointing to the fact that recalling God's past faithfulness helps us regain hope. When we pause to remember how God has been faithful to us in the past—how He has provided, protected, and guided us through tough times—we can find comfort in knowing that He will do it again. Reflecting on God's unchanging faithfulness breaks through the fog of worry and confusion and allows us to see the bigger picture: that God has always been with us, and He will never fail us.

The writer of Lamentations was experiencing deep sorrow and grief, much like the mental fog that can consume us when we're overwhelmed by life's challenges. But even in that darkness, he made a conscious choice to recall God's mercies. This act of remembering shifted his focus away from the present troubles and reminded him that God's compassion never fails. When our minds are clouded by confusion or worry, we can make that same choice. We can take a moment to remember all the times God has been faithful, all the times He has brought us through challenges that seemed impossible at the time. This practice of remembering can bring peace to our troubled minds because it reminds us that no matter how difficult things seem right now, God is still in control, and His mercy will carry us through.

Mental fog can often make us feel isolated, like we're carrying our burdens alone. But Lamentations 3:22 reminds us that "It is of the LORD's mercies that we are not consumed." In other words, it's God's mercy that sustains us and keeps us from being completely overwhelmed by life's struggles. Even when our minds are foggy and we can't see a way out, God's mercy is present, holding us together and giving us the strength to keep going. This truth is a powerful reminder that we are not alone in our struggles. God is with us, and His compassion never fails. Knowing this can help lift the mental fog because it reminds us that we don't have to have everything figured out on our own. God's faithfulness is unchanging, and His mercy is always available to us, even when we feel lost.

Another reason why recalling God's faithfulness is so important when your mind is in a fog is that it helps to shift your perspective. When you're overwhelmed, it's easy to get stuck in a cycle of negative thinking, where all you can see are the problems in front of you. But remembering how God has been faithful in the past helps you see beyond the current moment of confusion. It gives you hope that the fog will eventually lift and that God is working behind the scenes, even if you can't see it right now. Reflecting on God's past mercies gives you the strength to keep going, even when you're not sure what the next step should be. It helps you trust that, just as He has been faithful before, He will be faithful again.

Lamentations 3:21-22 speaks of God's mercies being new every morning, which is another powerful reminder when you're dealing with mental fog. Sometimes, when you're in the thick of confusion or stress, it can feel like the fog will never lift. But God's mercy is new every day, meaning that each day is a fresh opportunity for clarity, peace, and hope. No matter how overwhelming things might seem today, you can trust that God's compassion is available to you, and He will give you the strength and wisdom you need to face each new day. This realization can bring a sense of peace and help clear the fog because it reminds you that you're not stuck in this moment forever. God is always working, and He is always offering new mercies to help guide you through whatever challenges you're facing.

When you feel like your mind is in a fog, one of the most helpful things you can do is pause and remember the specific ways God has been faithful to you in the past. Think about the times when you were facing a difficult situation and God provided for you, or when you were uncertain about the future, and God made a way. Recalling these moments helps to break the cycle of worry and confusion because it reminds you that God has never failed you before, and He won't start now. This practice of remembering God's faithfulness helps to bring clarity to your mind because it shifts your focus away from the problems and onto the solution—God's unchanging mercy and compassion.

Lamentations 3:22 emphasizes that God's compassions "fail not," which is a comforting truth when you're feeling mentally or emotionally overwhelmed. No matter how foggy your mind feels or how difficult your circumstances may be, God's compassion is always available to you. He sees your struggles, and He cares deeply about what you're going through. His compassion never runs out, and He is always ready to offer you comfort, strength, and peace. When you remember this truth, it helps to clear the mental fog because it reassures you that you are not alone in your struggles. God's compassion is a constant, reliable source of comfort and hope, and it's available to you no matter what you're facing.

Reflecting on God's faithfulness also helps you cultivate a sense of gratitude, which is another powerful tool for clearing mental fog. When you're focused on your problems, it's easy to feel overwhelmed and discouraged. But when you take the time to remember all the ways God has been good to you, it shifts your perspective and helps you see things in a more positive light. Gratitude helps to lift the fog of worry and confusion because it reminds you of all the blessings you've received and the ways God has worked in your life. This shift in focus can bring a sense of peace and clarity that helps you move forward with a renewed sense of hope and purpose.

In moments of mental fog, it's important to remember that God's faithfulness is not dependent on your circumstances. Even when everything feels confusing or uncertain, God is still faithful. His compassion and mercy are not limited by the challenges you're facing. In fact, it's often in the most difficult times that we see God's faithfulness most clearly. When you're in the middle of mental fog, it can be hard to see how things will work out, but remembering God's faithfulness helps you trust that He is working, even when you can't see it. This trust brings a sense of peace that helps to clear the fog and gives you the strength to keep going.

In conclusion, when your mind is in a fog, and everything feels overwhelming, one of the most powerful things you can do is remember God's faithfulness. Lamentations 3:21-22 reminds us that recalling God's past mercies gives us hope and helps us see beyond the current moment of confusion. God's compassion never fails, and His mercies are new every morning. When you take the time to reflect on how God has been faithful to you in the past, it helps to bring clarity and peace to your mind. It reminds you that no matter how foggy things might seem right now, God is still in control, and His mercy will carry you through. Reflecting on God's unchanging faithfulness lifts the mental fog and gives you the strength and hope you need to move forward with confidence and trust in Him.

Chapter 9 - Managing Emotions

When your mind is in a fog, it often feels like your emotions are out of control. Fear, frustration, and anger can cloud your judgment and make it hard to think clearly. You might feel overwhelmed, as if your emotions are pulling you in different directions, leaving you unsure of what to do or how to respond. This emotional fog can be just as difficult to manage as mental fog because emotions, when not kept in check, can intensify the confusion and make everything seem more complicated than it really is. Proverbs 16:32 offers a key to dealing with this challenge, saying, "He that is slow to anger is better than the mighty; and he that ruleth his spirit than he that taketh a city." This verse highlights the importance of managing emotions, particularly the strong ones like anger and fear, because controlling our emotions allows us to think more clearly and make better decisions. In moments when your mind is in a fog, learning to manage your emotions can be the first step toward clearing the confusion and finding clarity again.

Emotions are a natural part of life, and everyone experiences them. But when emotions like anger or fear take over, they can cloud your ability to think rationally. Fear, for instance, can make even small problems seem enormous, while anger can lead you to make rash decisions that you might regret later. Proverbs 16:32 teaches us that controlling these emotions is a sign of real strength, greater even than physical power or external achievements like "taking a city." In other words, the ability to control your emotions is a skill that can help you navigate life's challenges more effectively than brute force or even cleverness. When you are able to rule your spirit, you are better equipped to handle the ups and downs of life, even when your mind feels foggy and unclear.

When your mind is foggy, it's easy to get caught up in emotional reactions. If something goes wrong, your first response might be anger or frustration, and this can cloud your judgment, making the situation feel even more overwhelming. But Proverbs 16:32 encourages us to be "slow to anger," reminding us that it's important to pause, take a breath, and think before reacting. By slowing down and not letting anger control your actions, you give yourself the opportunity to approach the situation with a clear mind. This can help you see things more objectively, rather than being swept away by your emotions.

One of the challenges of managing emotions when your mind is in a fog is that emotions often seem more intense during these times. When you're already feeling mentally overwhelmed, it's easier for small frustrations to feel like big problems. Something as simple as a minor inconvenience can trigger a much larger emotional reaction than it normally would, and this can spiral into more confusion and stress. Proverbs 16:32 teaches us that controlling our emotions, especially in these moments, is crucial because it helps us regain control over the situation. When you rule your spirit—meaning you don't let your emotions take over—you're able to step back, evaluate the situation more calmly, and respond in a way that brings peace rather than more chaos.

Fear is another emotion that can cloud your judgment when your mind is in a fog. Fear often makes problems seem bigger than they are, leading to a sense of panic or helplessness. But when you learn to manage your fear, you can face challenges with more confidence and clarity. Proverbs 16:32 reminds us that strength doesn't come from overpowering others or dominating situations; it comes from being able to control your own emotions and responses. When you rule your spirit, you're able to face fear without letting it take control. You can acknowledge that you're afraid, but you don't let that fear dictate your actions or cloud your judgment. This helps clear the mental fog because you're no longer being driven by fear, but instead, you're making thoughtful decisions based on what's really happening, not on what you're afraid might happen.

Managing emotions is a key part of finding clarity when your mind is in a fog, but it's not always easy. It takes practice and patience to learn how to be slow to anger and to rule your spirit, especially when you're feeling overwhelmed. But the more you practice controlling your emotions, the easier it becomes to stay calm and think clearly, even in stressful situations. Proverbs 16:32 offers a powerful reminder that emotional control is a form of strength, and it's a strength that can help you break through the mental fog that clouds your thinking.

One of the ways to manage your emotions is by developing self-awareness. When you're aware of your emotions—when you recognize that you're feeling angry, frustrated, or afraid—you can take steps to calm yourself before reacting. This is part of what it means to "rule your spirit." Instead of letting your emotions control you, you take control of your emotions by acknowledging them and choosing how to respond. For example, if you feel anger rising up, you can pause and take a few deep breaths before saying or doing something in response. This small act of controlling your reaction can prevent you from making decisions based on anger, which might only make the situation worse.

Another important aspect of managing emotions is learning to release them in healthy ways. Emotions like anger and fear are not inherently bad; they're natural responses to life's challenges. But when these emotions are not managed properly, they can cloud your mind and lead to confusion. Finding healthy ways to express and release your emotions—whether it's through talking to a friend, writing in a journal, or taking a walk—can help clear the mental fog. By letting go of the intense emotions in a constructive way, you free up mental space to think more clearly and make better decisions. Proverbs 16:32 encourages us to be "slow to anger," and part of being slow to anger is finding ways to release that anger before it takes control of your actions.

It's also important to remember that managing emotions doesn't mean ignoring them or pretending they don't exist. Emotions are real, and they deserve to be acknowledged. Proverbs 16:32 doesn't tell us to suppress our emotions; it tells us to control them. This means recognizing your emotions, understanding why you're feeling the way you do, and then choosing how to respond. When your mind is in a fog, it's easy to get swept up in your emotions without stopping to consider what's really going on. But when you take the time to acknowledge your emotions and think through them, you can prevent them from clouding your judgment.

Sometimes, managing emotions in the midst of mental fog requires help from others. Talking to a trusted friend, family member, or counselor can give you a new perspective on the situation and help you process your emotions in a healthy way. Proverbs 16:32 highlights the importance of ruling your spirit, but that doesn't mean you have to do it all on your own. Seeking guidance and support from others can help you stay grounded and give you the clarity you need to manage your emotions effectively.

Another key to managing emotions and clearing mental fog is to stay connected to God. Prayer and reflection can help you bring your emotions to God, asking Him for wisdom, peace, and clarity. When you're feeling overwhelmed by emotions, turning to God in prayer can help calm your mind and provide a sense of peace that allows you to think more clearly. Proverbs 16:32 reminds us that true strength comes from controlling our emotions, and this strength is something we can find in our relationship with God. Through prayer and reliance on God's guidance, we can learn to manage our emotions in a way that brings clarity, peace, and wisdom.

In moments of mental fog, it's easy to feel like your emotions are too strong to handle. But Proverbs 16:32 reminds us that we have the ability to control our emotions, and doing so is a form of strength that is greater than any physical power. When you're able to rule your spirit, you're better equipped to navigate life's challenges with a clear mind and a calm heart. Managing emotions doesn't mean you won't feel them, but it does mean you have the power to decide how you'll respond to them. This control brings clarity and helps to lift the fog that often clouds your thinking when emotions run high.

In conclusion, when your mind is in a fog and your emotions feel overwhelming, Proverbs 16:32 offers a powerful reminder of the importance of managing emotions. Being slow to anger and ruling your spirit are signs of true strength, and this strength helps you think more clearly and make better decisions, even in the midst of confusion. By learning to manage your emotions—whether it's fear, anger, or frustration—you can begin to clear the mental fog and find peace and clarity. This process takes practice, patience, and sometimes the support of others, but it's a skill that can bring immense benefits to your life. When you control your emotions, you're better able to navigate life's challenges with wisdom, calmness, and strength, and you can approach each day with a clearer mind and a more peaceful heart.

Chapter 10 - Mapping Out Your Thoughts

When your mind is in a fog, everything feels jumbled, and it's difficult to see clearly or make sense of what's going on. You might be dealing with stress, confusion, or worry, and all of these thoughts can swirl around in your head, making it harder and harder to focus. The mental fog can leave you feeling stuck and overwhelmed, as if no matter how hard you try, you can't seem to sort out your thoughts or figure out the next steps. This is where writing things down can be incredibly helpful. In Habakkuk 2:2, the Lord tells the prophet, "Write the vision, and make it plain upon tables, that he may run that readeth it." This simple yet powerful instruction highlights the importance of writing things out clearly so that we can understand and act on them. When you're in a mental fog, mapping out your thoughts by writing them down can bring much-needed clarity and direction, helping you break through the confusion and see the path forward more clearly.

One of the reasons mental fog is so difficult to deal with is that it creates a sense of chaos in your mind. You might have a thousand thoughts racing through your head—worries about the future, concerns about a problem you're facing, or decisions you need to make—and it can feel impossible to keep track of everything. This mental clutter makes it hard to focus on any one thing, and the more you try to sort through it, the more overwhelmed you might feel. But Habakkuk 2:2 shows us that writing things down can help bring order to the chaos. When you take the time to write out your thoughts, concerns, or plans, it's like organizing the clutter in your mind. Putting your thoughts down on paper allows you to see them more clearly, rather than having them all jumbled up in your head. Writing things down can give you a clearer sense of what's really going on, helping to lift the mental fog and bring you closer to understanding.

Writing is a powerful tool for clearing mental fog because it forces you to slow down and focus on one thing at a time. When your mind is foggy, it's easy to feel overwhelmed by the sheer number of things you need to think about or do. But when you sit down to write, you have to take each thought or concern and put it into words. This process helps you break things down into smaller, more manageable pieces. Instead of feeling like you have a mountain of problems to deal with, you can start to see each issue or thought more clearly and figure out how to address it. Habakkuk 2:2 encourages us to "make it plain," meaning that when we write things down, we should aim to be clear and straightforward. This clarity helps you understand what needs to be done and gives you a sense of direction, which can help lift the mental fog that's been clouding your mind.

Another reason why writing things down is so effective at clearing mental fog is that it helps you prioritize. When your mind is filled with too many thoughts, it's hard to know where to start or what to focus on first. But by writing things down, you can start to see which issues are most pressing and which ones can wait. This helps you prioritize your tasks or concerns, allowing you to focus on what's most important rather than trying to tackle everything at once. Habakkuk 2:2 says to "write the vision" and "make it plain," which implies that there's a specific goal or direction in mind. Writing things down helps you clarify that goal or vision, making it easier to prioritize your actions and decisions. Once you have a clear understanding of what's most important, the mental fog starts to lift because you're no longer trying to juggle everything in your head at once.

One of the greatest benefits of writing things down is that it helps you gain perspective. When your mind is foggy, it's easy to get lost in your thoughts and feel like you're drowning in problems. Everything can start to feel overwhelming, and you might lose sight of the bigger picture. But when you write things down, you can step back and see your thoughts from a different perspective. It's like taking a mental snapshot of what's going on in your head and putting it on paper, where you can look at it more objectively. This new perspective can help you see solutions or possibilities that you might not have noticed before. Habakkuk 2:2 tells us to "make it plain," and part of making something plain is being able to see it clearly. Writing things down helps you take a step back from the fog of confusion and look at your thoughts with fresh eyes, which can lead to greater understanding and clarity.

Writing can also be a way to release the emotions or worries that are contributing to your mental fog. Sometimes, when we're overwhelmed, it's because we're carrying too many emotional burdens that we haven't had a chance to process. Writing about how you're feeling—whether it's frustration, fear, sadness, or uncertainty—can be a way to get those emotions out of your head and onto paper. This process of releasing your emotions through writing can be incredibly freeing, and it often helps to clear the mental fog because it gives you space to breathe. Habakkuk 2:2 speaks of writing the vision and making it plain so that "he may run that readeth it." In a similar way, writing out your emotions and concerns can give you the mental clarity and emotional release you need to move forward. Once those feelings are out in the open, you're no longer carrying them around in your mind, which makes it easier to think clearly and focus on what's important.

Another important aspect of writing things down is that it creates a sense of accountability. When your thoughts are swirling around in your head, it's easy to lose track of what you need to do or forget important details. But when you write things down, you're creating a record that you can refer back to. This accountability helps you stay on track and follow through on your plans, which can bring a sense of control and order to your day. Habakkuk 2:2 talks about writing the vision so that "he may run that readeth it," suggesting that having a clear plan or direction helps you take action. When you write things down, you're not just organizing your thoughts—you're also setting yourself up for success by giving yourself a clear roadmap to follow. This accountability helps to lift the mental fog because it gives you a concrete plan to work from, rather than leaving everything floating around in your mind.

It's also worth noting that writing things down can help you track your progress. When your mind is in a fog, it's easy to feel like you're not getting anywhere, even if you're making small steps forward. Writing down your thoughts, plans, or goals allows you to see the progress you're making over time. This can be incredibly encouraging, especially when you're dealing with a difficult situation or trying to work through a complex problem. Habakkuk 2:2 emphasizes the importance of writing things down clearly so that you can understand and take action. By keeping a written record of your thoughts and progress, you can look back and see how far you've come, which can help clear the mental fog and give you the motivation to keep moving forward.

Finally, writing things down is a way to invite God into the process of clearing your mental fog. When you write out your thoughts, concerns, or plans, you're not just doing it for yourself—you're also opening up a space for God to speak to you. Writing can be a form of prayer, where you pour out your heart to God and ask for His guidance and wisdom. Habakkuk 2:2 speaks of writing the vision and making it plain, and when you write your thoughts down, you're giving God the opportunity to bring clarity and understanding to your situation. You might find that as you write, God reveals insights or solutions that you hadn't considered before. This process of writing and reflection can help to clear the mental fog and bring a sense of peace, knowing that God is with you and guiding you every step of the way.

In conclusion, when your mind is in a fog and you're struggling to find clarity, writing things down can be a powerful tool for bringing order and understanding to your thoughts. Habakkuk 2:2 encourages us to "write the vision, and make it plain," reminding us that writing things down helps to clarify our thoughts, prioritize our actions, and gain perspective. By mapping out your thoughts on paper, you can break through the mental fog and see the path forward more clearly. Writing not only helps you organize your thoughts, but it also provides a sense of accountability and progress, helping you stay on track and move forward with confidence. Whether you're dealing with stress, confusion, or uncertainty, writing things down can bring a sense of peace and clarity, allowing you to see God's hand at work in your life and trust that He is guiding you through the fog. So the next time your mind feels clouded, take a moment to write down your thoughts and concerns, and watch as the mental fog begins to lift, making way for clarity, understanding, and direction.

Chapter 11 - Mind Renewal

When your mind is in a fog, it feels like everything is blurry and confusing, like you're trying to walk through a thick mist without being able to see the path ahead. Thoughts become jumbled, it's hard to focus, and even the simplest decisions feel overwhelming. Whether this fog comes from stress, worry, fear, or just the busyness of life, it can be paralyzing, leaving you unsure of what to do next. But in Romans 12:2, we find a powerful key to clearing this mental fog: "And be not conformed to this world: but be ye transformed by the renewing of your mind, that ye may prove what is that good, and acceptable, and perfect, will of God." This verse speaks directly to the process of renewing our minds, a crucial step in gaining clarity when everything feels overwhelming. When we renew our minds, we allow God's Word to clear out the confusion and help us align our thoughts with His perfect will. It's like wiping away the foggy mist and seeing the clear, bright path that God has set before us.

Mental fog can come from all sorts of places—stress at school or work, worries about the future, or the pressures of daily life. The world around us is constantly pulling at our attention, filling our minds with distractions, negative thoughts, and fears. When we get caught up in these things, it's easy to lose sight of what truly matters, and our minds become cluttered with the noise of the world. This is why Romans 12:2 tells us not to be "conformed to this world." When we conform to the world, we allow its chaos, worries, and distractions to take over our minds. The result is mental fog—a state where our thoughts are clouded, and we can't think clearly. But God doesn't want us to live in confusion.

Instead, He calls us to be "transformed by the renewing of [our] mind." This transformation comes when we choose to focus on God's Word and His will for our lives, rather than the noise of the world. It's through this renewal that we find clarity, peace, and direction.

The idea of renewing the mind is like pressing a reset button. When your computer is overloaded with too many tasks, it starts to slow down, and sometimes it even freezes. In these moments, you might need to restart it to clear out the unnecessary programs and give it a fresh start. Our minds can be similar. When we're overloaded with too many worries, distractions, or negative thoughts, our mental capacity becomes overwhelmed, and we feel stuck. Renewing the mind is God's way of helping us reset. By focusing on His Word, we allow Him to clear out the clutter, the fears, and the confusion, and replace them with His truth. This process brings a sense of peace and clarity that cuts through the mental fog and helps us see things more clearly.

Romans 12:2 tells us that renewing the mind is a transformative process. It's not just about thinking differently for a moment; it's about experiencing a deep, lasting change in the way we approach life. This transformation happens when we stop conforming to the patterns of the world—the patterns of worry, fear, and distraction—and start focusing on God's will. The world might tell us to worry about the future, to stress over things we can't control, or to constantly chase after things that don't really matter. But when we renew our minds by focusing on God's Word, we learn to let go of these things. We begin to trust in God's plan, knowing that His will for us is good, acceptable, and perfect. This trust brings a sense of peace that lifts the mental fog and allows us to move forward with confidence.

One of the key ways to renew the mind is through daily meditation on Scripture. Just as we need to eat healthy food to nourish our bodies, we need to feed our minds with God's truth to keep them clear and focused. When we meditate on God's Word, we remind ourselves of His promises, His love, and His plan for our lives. This helps to push out the negative thoughts and worries that cloud our minds and replace them with thoughts of peace, hope, and faith. Over time, this practice of renewing the mind through Scripture transforms the way we think. Instead of being overwhelmed by the things of the world, we become anchored in God's truth, which gives us the clarity and strength we need to face whatever challenges come our way.

Another important aspect of mind renewal is prayer. When we're feeling overwhelmed or confused, prayer is a powerful way to bring our thoughts and worries to God and ask for His guidance. In prayer, we can be honest with God about the mental fog we're experiencing, and we can ask Him to help us see things more clearly. As we spend time in prayer, God often brings clarity to our minds, helping us to see the situation from His perspective. He reminds us of His faithfulness and His control over our lives, which helps to calm our fears and clear the fog of confusion. Prayer is not just about asking for things; it's about aligning our hearts and minds with God's will. When we do this, we open ourselves up to the renewing work that God wants to do in our minds.

Romans 12:2 also reminds us that the purpose of mind renewal is to "prove what is that good, and acceptable, and perfect, will of God." When our minds are clouded by the world's distractions, it's hard to know what God's will is for our lives. But as we renew our minds by focusing on His Word and His truth, we begin to see things more clearly. We start to understand what God's will is for us in each situation, and this gives us the direction we need to move forward. Knowing God's will brings a sense of peace and purpose that clears away the mental fog. Instead of feeling lost or unsure, we can move forward with confidence, knowing that we are walking in God's plan for our lives.

Mental fog can often make us feel stuck, like we're spinning our wheels but not getting anywhere. But when we renew our minds by focusing on God's truth, we start to see the path forward more clearly. We gain a sense of direction and purpose that helps us break free from the confusion and uncertainty. Renewing the mind is about shifting our focus away from the things that don't matter—the worries, the fears, the distractions—and focusing instead on the things that do matter: God's love, His promises, and His will for our lives. This shift in focus is what clears the mental fog and allows us to move forward with clarity and peace.

Another important aspect of renewing the mind is letting go of negative thought patterns. The world is full of negativity—fear of the future, doubt about our abilities, and constant comparisons to others. These negative thoughts can easily take root in our minds, creating a fog of self-doubt and fear. But Romans 12:2 reminds us that we don't have to conform to these patterns. Through mind renewal, we can replace these negative thoughts with the truth of who we are in Christ. God's Word tells us that we are loved, chosen, and equipped for every good work. When we meditate on these truths, it helps to break the cycle of negative thinking and replace it with thoughts of hope, confidence, and faith. This is a key part of clearing the mental fog and experiencing the transformation that comes from renewing our minds.

It's also important to remember that mind renewal is a daily process. Just as our minds can become cluttered with new worries and distractions each day, we need to renew our minds daily by returning to God's Word and His truth. It's not a one-time event, but a continuous journey of transformation. Each day, we have the opportunity to refocus our thoughts on God's will and allow Him to clear away the mental fog. This daily renewal helps us stay grounded in God's truth, no matter what challenges or distractions come our way.

In conclusion, when your mind is in a fog and you're struggling to find clarity, Romans 12:2 offers a powerful solution: the renewal of the mind. By focusing on God's Word and His will for our lives, we can clear away the confusion, worry, and distractions that cloud our thinking. Renewing the mind is a transformative process that helps us align our thoughts with God's perfect plan, giving us the clarity and direction we need to move forward with confidence. Through daily meditation on Scripture, prayer, and the intentional replacement of negative thoughts with God's truth, we can experience the peace and clarity that comes from a renewed mind. As we continue this process of mind renewal, we are better equipped to "prove what is that good, and acceptable, and perfect, will of God" for our lives, and we can walk in His purpose with a clear mind and a peaceful heart.

Chapter 12 - Move in Faith

When your mind is in a fog, it's like trying to navigate through a dense mist where you can't see clearly, and every step forward feels uncertain. You may feel overwhelmed by decisions, confused about the future, or unsure of how to move forward in the challenges you're facing. This fog of confusion can leave you feeling stuck, as if you're trapped in a place where everything is unclear and nothing seems certain. But in times like these, the Bible offers us a simple yet powerful reminder in 2 Corinthians 5:7, "For we walk by faith, not by sight." This verse reminds us that even when we can't see the way forward, even when life feels overwhelming and unclear, we can still move forward with confidence by trusting in God and walking in faith. Faith is the key that helps us take steps in the right direction, even when the path ahead seems hidden in a fog.

The world teaches us to rely on what we can see, touch, and understand with our human senses. We are often told to wait until we have all the answers or until things make sense before taking action. But this approach can leave us paralyzed when our minds are clouded with doubt, fear, or uncertainty. In these moments of mental fog, waiting for everything to become clear before moving forward is often not possible. This is where walking by faith comes in. Faith means trusting in God's promises and believing that He is guiding you, even when you can't see the full picture. It's about relying on God's wisdom rather than your own understanding, and trusting that He will lead you through the fog, one step at a time.

Walking by faith is not about ignoring reality or pretending that everything is easy. Instead, it's about acknowledging that life is often filled with uncertainty and challenges, but choosing to trust in God's faithfulness regardless. It's recognizing that while your mind might be clouded with confusion, God sees the bigger picture and knows the way forward. Faith helps you take that next step, even when you can't see exactly where it will lead. It allows you to move forward with confidence, not because you have all the answers, but because you trust in the One who does.

In times of mental fog, it's easy to feel like you're stuck in place, unsure of how to make progress. You might be waiting for a moment of clarity, hoping that the fog will suddenly lift and reveal the answers you're searching for. But the truth is, sometimes clarity comes only after we take steps of faith. As 2 Corinthians 5:7 tells us, "For we walk by faith, not by sight." This means that even when things aren't perfectly clear, even when you don't know exactly what the future holds, you can still move forward, trusting that God will guide you. Faith often requires us to step out, even when we don't have all the details figured out. And as we walk in faith, trusting God with each step, the fog begins to lift, and the path ahead becomes clearer.

Think of walking by faith like driving in a thick fog at night. Your car's headlights can only illuminate a few feet ahead of you, and beyond that, everything is hidden in darkness. But even though you can't see the entire road, you keep moving forward because you trust that the road is there and that your car will take you where you need to go. Faith works in much the same way. You might not be able to see the whole path ahead, but you trust that God is leading you and that He knows where you're going. Each step of faith brings you a little closer to clarity, and though you might not see the entire picture, you have enough light to take the next step.

One of the reasons why walking by faith is so powerful is because it shifts our focus away from our own limitations and places it on God's limitless power. When you're in a mental fog, it's easy to become consumed by your own doubts and uncertainties. You might feel like you're not strong enough, smart enough, or capable enough to handle the challenges in front of you. But faith reminds you that it's not about your own abilities; it's about trusting in God's strength and wisdom. When you walk by faith, you're relying on God to make a way, even when you can't see how things will work out. This trust in God helps to clear the mental fog, because it frees you from the pressure of having to figure everything out on your own.

Another important aspect of walking by faith is surrendering control. Mental fog often comes from trying to control every aspect of life, worrying about every possible outcome, and overthinking decisions. But faith requires surrender—it's about letting go of the need to control everything and trusting that God's plan is better than your own. When you walk by faith, you're saying, "God, I don't have all the answers, and I can't see the whole path, but I trust that You do, and I'm willing to follow where You lead." This act of surrender helps to clear the mental fog, because it releases the weight of trying to manage everything on your own and allows you to rest in the assurance that God is in control.

Faith also brings a sense of peace that helps to lift the fog of confusion. When you're walking by sight—relying solely on what you can see or understand—it's easy to feel anxious or uncertain when things don't go as planned. But when you walk by faith, you have the peace of knowing that God is with you, guiding your steps and working everything out for your good, even when you can't see how. This peace comes from trusting in God's promises, knowing that He is faithful and that He will never leave you or forsake you. As you walk by faith, this peace begins to replace the confusion and uncertainty, helping to clear your mind and bring clarity to the situation.

Walking by faith also requires perseverance. Sometimes, the fog doesn't lift right away. You might take a step of faith and still feel like you're walking through uncertainty. But faith isn't about having instant answers—it's about trusting God enough to keep moving forward, even when the path ahead is still unclear. The more you walk in faith, the stronger your trust in God becomes, and the more confident you become in His ability to guide you through the fog. Each step of faith builds on the last, and over time, the fog begins to lift as you grow in your confidence in God's plan for your life.

One of the beautiful things about walking by faith is that it invites God to work in ways that we might never expect. When you walk by sight—when you only move forward based on what you can see or understand—you limit yourself to what's within your control. But when you walk by faith, you open yourself up to the incredible things that God can do. Sometimes, God's plan for our lives is bigger and better than anything we could imagine, but we only experience it when we step out in faith and trust Him to lead us. Walking by faith allows us to experience the fullness of God's plan, even when we can't see the full picture.

In moments of mental fog, it can be tempting to stand still, waiting for everything to make sense before taking action. But 2 Corinthians 5:7 encourages us to walk by faith, not by sight. This means that we don't have to wait for all the answers before moving forward. We can trust that God is guiding us, even when the way isn't perfectly clear. As we take steps of faith, God often reveals the next steps, one at a time. And as we keep walking, the path becomes clearer, and the fog begins to lift.

It's also important to remember that faith is not something we have to muster up on our own. Faith is a gift from God, and it grows as we spend time in His Word, prayer, and reflection. When you're feeling mentally foggy and unsure of how to move forward, spending time in Scripture can strengthen your faith and remind you of God's promises. Reading stories of how God has guided His people in the past, reflecting on His faithfulness in your own life, and praying for His guidance can help build your faith, giving you the confidence to take the next step, even when the way forward isn't fully clear.

In conclusion, when your mind is in a fog and you're struggling to find clarity, 2 Corinthians 5:7 offers a powerful reminder that we walk by faith, not by sight. Even when we can't see the full picture, we can trust that God is guiding us and that He knows the way forward. Walking by faith means taking steps of trust, even when the path is hidden in a fog of uncertainty. It means surrendering control, relying on God's strength, and trusting in His promises. As we walk by faith, the fog begins to lift, and we gain a clearer sense of direction and peace. Faith doesn't require us to have all the answers—it requires us to trust in the One who does. By moving in faith, even when we can't see the way forward clearly, we open ourselves up to the incredible work that God is doing in our lives, and we experience the peace and clarity that comes from trusting in Him.

Conclusion

As we come to the end of this journey, it's important to remember that the fog of life—whether it's confusion, uncertainty, or overwhelming stress—is something we all face at different points. But the beauty of our walk with the Lord is that we are never left to face it alone. God's Word provides the foundation for clearing the fog, renewing our minds, and restoring our focus on Him. Through the pages of this book, we have explored the scriptural support God offers, showing us how to trust Him when we can't see the way forward and how to find clarity in His promises when our minds feel clouded.

Remember, just as we have seen in Romans 12:2, renewing our minds is an ongoing process. It requires daily intentionality to focus on God's truth and to allow His Word to shape our thoughts, attitudes, and decisions. The fog doesn't always disappear overnight, but as we continually seek God, meditate on His promises, and surrender our worries to Him, we will find that the path becomes clearer with each step of faith.

The key to navigating the fog is found in maintaining your walk with the Lord. It's easy to let distractions, fears, and worldly pressures pull you away from the still, small voice of God. But the challenge—and invitation—for you now is to cultivate a daily habit of staying connected to Him. Begin each day with prayer, asking for His guidance, wisdom, and peace. Dive into His Word, using it as the lamp to light your path, just as Psalm 119:105 reminds us: "Thy word is a lamp unto my feet, and a light unto my path."

In times when the fog of life feels thick, remember that 2 Corinthians 5:7 calls us to "walk by faith, not by sight." You may not always see the full picture, and you may not have all the answers, but God does. Faith is what allows you to take the next step, trusting that He is in control. Even when your mind feels overwhelmed, you can rest in the truth that God's love, mercy, and direction are steady and unchanging.

So, how do you continue in your walk with the Lord when the fog returns? The challenge is to be persistent in your pursuit of Him, even when clarity isn't immediate. When confusion creeps in, remind yourself of the truths you have learned in this book: God is your refuge, His Word is your guide, and His presence is your constant source of strength. Keep returning to Him in prayer, continually seeking His will above all else, and don't be afraid to be still and listen for His voice.

My final challenge to you is to embrace each foggy moment as an opportunity to deepen your faith. Let the moments of uncertainty draw you closer to the Lord, trusting that He is working in ways you cannot yet see. As you walk with Him, you will find that the fog begins to lift, and you will be led into a place of clarity, peace, and purpose. Trust in God's perfect timing and know that He is always with you, guiding you every step of the way. Keep walking in faith, and the fog will not define you—God's presence and His promises will.

Don't miss out!

Visit the website below and you can sign up to receive emails whenever Joshua Rhoades publishes a new book. There's no charge and no obligation.

https://books2read.com/r/B-A-AJLBB-QQRAF

BOOKS 2 READ

Connecting independent readers to independent writers.

Did you love *My Mind Is In A Fog What Do I Do??* Then you should read *Anchored In Truth Exploring The Depths of Psalm 119*[1] by Joshua Rhoades!

[2]

"Anchored in Truth: Exploring the Depths of Psalm 119" is an invitation to dive into one of the Bible's most profound passages, offering a deep exploration of faith, devotion, and the transformative power of God's Word. As the longest chapter in the Bible, Psalm 119 is a masterpiece of spiritual expression, structured as an intricate acrostic with each section beginning with a letter of the Hebrew alphabet. This psalm is not just a collection of verses; it is a meditation on the beauty and necessity of God's law. Through its 176 verses, the psalmist reveals a fervent love for God's commandments, a deep dependence on His guidance, and an unyielding pursuit of understanding and wisdom found only in the Scriptures.

"Anchored in Truth" invites you to explore the rich themes of Psalm 119, offering insights into how God's Word can shape, guide, and sustain a life of faith. This book is crafted not just to help you understand the words of this ancient psalm but to experience them in a way that profoundly impacts your daily walk with God. As you journey through

---

1. https://books2read.com/u/mvPayX

2. https://books2read.com/u/mvPayX

each section, you will see how the psalmist's experiences resonate with the challenges and triumphs of your own spiritual life—whether it's seeking deliverance in trials, finding delight in God's statutes, or pleading for divine guidance.

This book is more than an intellectual study; it is a call to transformation. Psalm 119 urges us to anchor our lives in the unchanging truth of God's Word, making it the foundation of our character, decisions, and ultimate hope. The psalmist's devotion to God's law reminds us that Scripture is not just a set of rules or a historical text; it is the living Word of God, active and relevant in every aspect of our lives.

"Anchored in Truth" aims to inspire you to cultivate a deeper love for God's Word, seek His guidance in all things, and live out the truths found in these verses. As you read, may you be encouraged to stand firm in the faith, anchored in the unshakable truths of God's Word, and experience the wisdom, peace, and joy that come from living in alignment with His eternal commands.